T0130357

THE BIBLE BOOK OF GENESIS FOR CHILDREN "CREATION"

GENESIS
CHAPTERS 1 AND 2

WRITTEN AND ILLUSTRATED BY

Elizabeth Johnson

WestBow Press books may be ordered through booksellers or by contacting:

WestBow Press
A Division of Thomas Nelson & Zondervan
1663 Liberty Drive
Bloomington, IN 47403
www.westbowpress.com
1 (866) 928-1240

ISBN: 978-1-9736-7239-5 (sc)
ISBN: 978-1-9736-7240-1 (e)

Library of Congress Control Number: 2019912179

Print information available on the last page.

WestBow Press rev. date: 01/03/2020

WestBow
PRESS®
A DIVISION OF THOMAS NELSON
& ZONDERVAN

Dedication

To LC for all your love, help and support.
To LaMark, Madison and Matthew my Sweetie Pies
and little warriors for Christ.

GENESIS
CHAPTER 1

First Day

In the beginning of the world God (Elohim, God of power Who always existed) created, made from nothing the heavens and the earth.

The earth had no shape and was empty. The earth was also dark and mixed with deep waters.

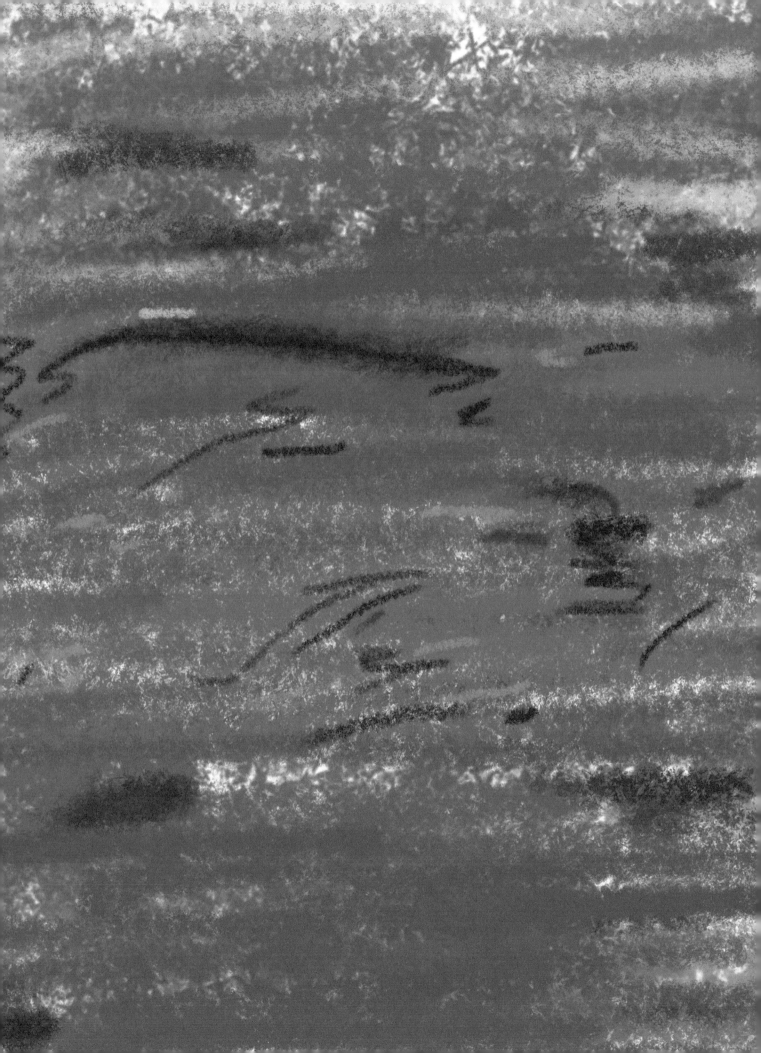

The Spirit, the breath and power of God moved over the deep waters. And God said, "Let there be light" and by God's spoken Word, bright beautiful light appeared.

And God looked at the light and saw that the light was good. And God separated the light from the darkness.

And God called the light Daytime and the darkness Nighttime. And there was evening and there was morning the first day.

Second Day

And God said, "Let there be a long empty space called a firmament in the middle of the waters and let the long empty space, the firmament, separate the waters."

And God made the long empty space, the firmament, and separated the waters so that some waters were under the firmament and some waters were above the firmament. And it happened just as God said.

And God called this long empty space, the firmament, Heaven. And there was evening and there was morning the second day.

Third Day

· ·

And God said, "Let the waters under the firmament, the Heaven, be gathered all in one place so that the waters may flow into many seas and let the dry land appear." And it happened as God said.

And God called the dry land Earth. And God called the gathering of the waters Seas. And God looked at the Earth and the Seas and saw that what He created was good.

And God said, "Let the earth produce grass and herbs with seeds to make more grass and herbs just like it, and fruit trees that give fruit with seeds to make more fruit trees just like it." And it happened just as God said.

The earth produced grass and herbs with seeds to make more grass and herbs just like it. And the earth produced fruit trees to give fruit with seeds to make more fruit trees just like it. And God looked at the grass and herb with seeds and the fruit trees with fruit with seeds and saw that what He created was good.

And there was evening and there was morning the third day.

Fourth Day

And God said, "Let there be lights in the firmament, the Heaven to separate the daytime from the nighttime, and let these lights be for signs from God that tell if it will rain or sunshine, and to tell the seasons, winter, spring, summer or fall, and that tell of the number of days and years, and that give light to the earth." And it happened just as God said.

And God made two great lights. The greater light, the Sun was to rule over and have power over the daytime and the lesser light, the Moon was to rule over and have power over the nighttime. God made the stars also to help light the earth. And God put these lights in the firmament, called Heaven in their place.

To give the earth light.

To rule over and have power over the daytime and over the nighttime.

To separate the light of the day from the darkness of the night.

And God looked at the lights that He put in their place in the firmament, called Heaven, and God saw that what he created was good.

And there was evening and there was morning the fourth day.

Fifth Day

And God said, "Let the waters produce many, many fish and other moving creatures that have life. And let the waters produce feathered and winged birds that may fly above the earth in the open firmament called Heaven."

And God created fish and great whales and every living creature that moves and has life in the waters to make many, many more like their own kind. And God created feathered and winged birds to make many, many more like their own kind.

And God looked at the fish and other living creatures in the waters and God looked at the feathered and winged birds that may fly in the firmament, called Heaven and God saw that what He created was good.

And God blessed the fish and other living creatures in the waters and gave them power and told them to produce many, many more fish and other living creatures and fill the waters in the seas. And God blessed, the feathered and winged birds that may fly in the firmament, called Heaven and gave them power and told them to produce many, many more feathered and winged birds and fill the earth.

And there was evening and there was morning the fifth day.

Sixth Day

And God said, "Let the earth produce wild animals like lions and elephants to make more wild animals like their own kind. And let the earth produce cattle and livestock to make more cattle and livestock like their own kind. And let the earth produce animals that move along the ground, creeping things to make more animals that move along the ground, creeping things like their own kind." And it happened just as God said.

And God made the wild animals of the earth like lions and elephants to make more like their own kind, and cattle and livestock to make more like their own kind, and animals that move along the ground, creeping things to make more like their own kind. And God looked at the wild animals like lions and elephants, and at the cattle and livestock and at the animals that move along the ground, creeping things and God saw that what He created was good.

And God said, "Let us (God the Father, God the Son, and God the Holy Spirit) make man (mankind, people) in our own image in our likeness. Let us make man (mankind, people) to be different from all other living creatures. Let us make mankind to be able to love and talk to God and listen to God. Let man (mankind) rule over and have power over the fish of the sea and over the feathered and winged birds of the air, and over the wild animals of the earth like lions and elephants, and over cattle and other livestock, and over animals that move along the ground, every creeping thing that creep upon the earth."

So, God created man (mankind, people) in his own image and likeness different from all other living creatures able to love and talk to God and listen to God. God created man (mankind, people) male and female, man and woman.

And God blessed them and gave them power and said to the man and woman to produce many, many more like their own kind to cover the earth and to rule over and have power over the earth and over the fish of the sea and over the feathered and winged birds of the air and over every living animal that moves on the earth.

And God said, "Behold, look and see, I have given you, man and woman every herb and plant with seed and every tree with fruit in which there is seed, on the earth for your food. And I have also given every animal of the earth and feathered and winged bird of the air and every animal that creeps along the earth with life, every herb and plant for food. "

And it happened just as God said.

And God looked and saw everything that He had made and behold (look and see) everything God created was **very** good.

And there was evening and there was morning the sixth day.

GENESIS
CHAPTER 2

Seventh Day

Just as God said and did, the firmament called Heaven was made with all that God created in it, light and sun, moon and stars. And the earth was made with all that God created in it, seas, plants and animals and mankind. And all was finished.

And on the seventh day God ended His work which He had made. And God rested on the seventh day from all His work which He had made.

And God blessed and gave power to the seventh day and made the seventh day holy to be used for mankind to rest, love, walk and talk with God, because on this day He rested from all His work which He created and made.

First Man Adam

This is the record of the making of the heavens and the earth, when they were created by the Lord God in the days that He made them. God is now called the Lord God (Who always existed without help from anyone or anything, the God who finished everything with His power, just as He said).

Now the Lord God made every plant before it was grown on the earth. And the Lord God made every herb before it grew on the earth; because the Lord God had not caused it to rain upon the earth and there was no man on the earth to work and care for the ground. But the Lord God sent up tiny drops of water from the earth to water the ground of the earth so that plants and trees and herbs could grow.

And the Lord God shaped and formed the body of man from the dust of the ground. And the Lord God breathed into the nostrils (the nose) of the man the breath of life from the Lord God and the man became alive, a living man with the breath of life of the Lord God.

And the Lord God planted a garden in Eden, the delightful place, and here he put the man who the Lord God had formed from the ground and breathed life into.

And out of the ground in the garden, Eden, a delightful place the Lord God made to grow every tree that was beautiful to look at and good for food. Also, in the middle of the garden there was the Tree of Life and the Tree of Knowing Good and Evil (bad).

And a river flowed out of Eden, the delightful place, to water the garden. And the river divided and became four rivers.

The first river was called Pi'son. The Pi'son River surrounded a land called Hav'ilah where there is gold and precious stoned.

The second river is called Gi'hon. The Gi'hon river surrounded a land called Ethiopia.

The third river was called Hid'dekel. The Hid'dekel River flows toward a land called Assyria.

The fourth river was called Euphra'tes.

And the Lord God took the man and put him in the garden in Eden, the delightful place to work and care for the garden.

The Beasts Are Formed

And the Lord God commanded, gave orders to the man saying, "You may eat freely of every tree in the garden, but you may not eat of the tree of Knowing Good and Evil (bad) because when you eat of this tree you will not continue to live (you will die)."

And the Lord God said, "It is not good for the man to be alone by himself, I will make a helper that is good for him." And from out of the ground, the Lord God shaped and formed every animal and every wild beast of the field and every feathered and winged bird of the air. And the Lord God brought every animal, wild beast and every feathered and winged bird before Adam so that Adam could give them names. And the names Adam gave to the animals, beasts and feathered and winged birds became their names. But among all the animals, beasts and feathered and winged birds, there was no helper that was good for Adam.

First Woman Is Made

So the Lord God caused the man, Adam to fall into a deep sleep and the Lord God took one of Adam's bones from his side and made a woman, a helper that was good for Adam and brought the woman to Adam.

And Adam said, "The Lord God made my helper from the bone of my body. She shall be called woman because she was made from man."

Therefore, a man shall leave his home, father and mother and be joined to his wife and the man and his wife shall become one, united together. And the man and the woman were not clothed because clothes were not needed in the Garden of Eden, the delightful place because the glory light of God covered them.

This is the first Book of the Bible, the Book of Genesis, Chapters One and Two.

This is the book of the Bible of when God created the heaven and the earth and all that was in it. God created the heavens, the earth, the animals and mankind and said all was **very** good.

All God created was **perfect** in the beginning when God created the heavens and the earth!

Printed in the United States
By Bookmasters